Welcome to Our World

A Guide to Tradition and Identity

Table of Contents

1. Introduction 2

2. Exploring the Notion of Tradition and Identity 3

    2.1. The Essence of Tradition 3

    2.2. Identity: An Intricate Tapestry 4

    2.3. Tradition and Identity: The Dance of Interplay 4

    2.4. Balancing Tradition, Identity, and Change 5

3. Defining Culture: An Introspective Analysis 7

    3.1. Unraveling the Complex Term: Culture 7

    3.2. The Multitudes of Culture: Tangible and Intangible ... 8

    3.3. Dimensions of Culture: The Iceberg Metaphor 8

    3.4. Culture and Identity: A Symbiotic Relationship 9

    3.5. An Ongoing Dialogue: Culture in an Evolving World ... 9

4. Symbols of Identity: Artifacts, Scripts, and Monuments ... 11

    4.1. Artifacts: Echoes of the Past 11

    4.2. Scripts: The Abstract Medium of Expression 12

    4.3. Monuments: Silent Narrators of Epochs 12

5. Festivities and Rituals: Expressions of Collective Tradition ... 14

    5.1. Celebration - A Universal Impulse 14

    5.2. Rituals - Patterns of Practice 15

    5.3. The Role of Festivities and Rituals 15

    5.4. Transformation and Continuity 16

    5.5. Future of Festivities and Rituals 16

6. Dance and Music: A Universal Language of Unity 18

    6.1. Dance and Music as Integral Parts of Ancient Cultures ... 18

    6.2. Music: Melodic Expression of the Soul 19

    6.3. Promoting Understanding and Empathy 20

7. Traditional Gastronomy: A Revealing Lens into Cultural Diversity ... 21

7.1. The Roots of Gastronomy ... 21

7.2. The Tapestry of Traditional Cuisines ... 21

7.3. Culinary Practices and Rituals: Stories Behind the Plate ... 22

7.4. The Spice Trade: A Story of Cultural Interactions ... 23

7.5. Traditional Gastronomy: Ecology and Sustainability ... 23

7.6. Securing Gastronomy's Future: Challenges & Resolutions ... 23

8. Language and Literature: Carriers of Cultural Identity ... 25

8.1. On the Cultural Implications of Language ... 25

8.2. Literature: A Reflection of Cultural Nuances ... 26

8.3. The Interplay of Language and Literature ... 26

8.4. Language Disruption, Endangerment, and Revitalization ... 27

8.5. Literature's Role in Preserving Cultural Identity ... 27

9. Traditional Clothing: A Tapestry of Time and Identity ... 29

9.1. The Significance of attire: An Intimate Connection to Identity ... 29

9.2. Evolution of Traditional Clothing: Chronicles from the Hands of Time ... 29

9.3. The Vocabulary of Colors and Motifs ... 30

9.4. Championing Local Material: A Testament to Geographic Conditions and Innovation ... 30

9.5. Traditional Clothing as Socioeconomic Indicators ... 31

9.6. The Modern Age: Catalyst of Changes and Adaptations ... 31

9.7. Preserving Traditional Clothing: An Imperative Task ... 31

10. Clash and Fusion: The Impact of Globalization on Traditions ... 33

10.1. The Onrush of Globalization ... 33

10.2. Tradition Clash: The Rumble of Cultures ... 34

10.3. Tradition Fusion: The Melting Pot of Globalization ... 34

10.4. The Fine Balance ... 35

10.5. The Unfolding Chapter ... 35

11. A Cultural Voyage: Preserving Tradition and Identity for the

Future 36

11.1. The Peril of Global Homogenization 36

11.2. The Power of Modern Technologies 37

11.3. Grassroots Movements and Institutional Support 37

11.4. The Role of Education 38

11.5. Shaping the Future with Tradition and Identity 38

Culture is the widening of the mind and of the spirit.

Chapter 1. Introduction

Dive into our riveting Special Report, "Welcome to Our World: A Guide to Tradition and Identity" - a panoramic exploration of diverse cultures, glorious traditions, and compelling identities that intricately shape our world and its people. This vibrant tapestry of insights will transport you on a heart-stirring journey, revealing how our customs and beliefs bind us together as a global community. Perfect for the curious at heart, culture enthusiasts, or anyone yearning to deepen their understanding of humanity, this Special Report will expand your horizons and fuel your sense of wonder. By delving into this extraordinary compilation, you're not just purchasing a report, but securing a passport to the vast, colorful, and deeply rooted traditions of our world, unveiling humanity in its most authentic form!

Chapter 2. Exploring the Notion of Tradition and Identity

In our pursuit of understanding, let us dive into the vast yet intricate concepts of 'tradition' and 'identity'. These two words, though seemingly regular, carry immense depth and evoke a multitude of interpretations, varying greatly depending on the individual, community, or context. They fashion the scaffolding that forms our worldview, shape communities, and, ultimately, fashion the cultural landscape of our globe.

2.1. The Essence of Tradition

Tradition - the term itself derives from the Latin word 'tradere', which means to transmit, hand over, to give for safekeeping. It refers largely to the transmission of customs or beliefs from generation to generation. Businesses continue long-standing practices, families pass down looms, tribes dictate rules of life—from the moment of birth to that of death, the footprints of tradition echo in the corridors of time.

Traditions exist in myriad forms, spanning various aspects of our lives. Some are sacrosanct rites that trace back to antiquity, whereas others may be mere habitual actions reincarnated daily, such as a morning cup of tea or reading at bedtime. Regardless, each tradition we subscribe to serves as a thread in the intricate fabric of societal continuity, knitting generations together across the span of history.

However, a significant aspect of understanding tradition requires us to venture beyond its surface value. When one deeply introspects a tradition, it is found to be intimately associated with a deeper cultural or societal value. The rituals of tradition, then, become performative expressions of a collective commitment to these values. Beyond exercising a sense of comfort and familiarity, traditions, therefore, serve to reinforce the philosophies we collectively choose to embrace and propagate.

2.2. Identity: An Intricate Tapestry

Moving from the collective to the individual, we approach the expansive concept of 'identity'. Identity—an introspective construct—is the way one perceives oneself or the manner in which one is perceived by others. Seemingly simple, identity is, in fact, a complex amalgamation of a multitude of factors including but not restricted to gender, ethnicity, religion, profession, hobbies, or geographical location. But the real complexity of identity lies in its dynamic nature—it evolves as we evolve, shaped and molded by the experiences we encounter.

A tangible facet of identity often takes form in the 'symbols of identity', woven into everyday life. These symbols could range from language, clothing, cuisine, and artifacts to more abstract concepts like shared histories, values, or practices. In essence, these elements bridge the divide between personal and collective reality—encoding individuality within a collective context.

2.3. Tradition and Identity: The Dance of Interplay

Having explored the depths of both tradition and identity, it is now time to delve into the essence of their relationship. A dance of delicate interplay, tradition and identity are two strands that weave the global tapestry of human society.

The influence of tradition on identity is not difficult to observe—the customs and beliefs passed down through generations majorly sculpt the individual and collective identity. Be it through celebrating a particular holiday, or embracing certain societal norms, traditions lay a robust, often unconscious, foundation for identity formation.

Conversely, the impact of evolving identities on traditions is also substantial—existing traditions may change or evolve as the community's identity evolves, as communities respond to changes in perception, environment, knowledge, or societal structure. This dynamicism infuses vitality in societal patterns, providing room for both continuity and innovation—ultimately, perpetuating human cultural diversity.

2.4. Balancing Tradition, Identity, and Change

A pertinent issue in discussions involving tradition and identity involves the balancing act of change. The world around us is ever-evolving, and humans, being adaptable entities, constantly evolve their worldview. When faced with this inevitability of change, how does the relationship between tradition and identity translate?

In essence, it's a process of continuous negotiation. Tradition retains relevance when it aligns with the current identity narratives, and at times when it doesn't, it either adapts or is discarded. Similarly, as identity shifts—so does our understanding and interpretation of tradition.

In conclusion, the exploration of tradition and identity reveals an intricate and interwoven dance of concepts that continually shape the human experience. As we peel back the layers, we begin to appreciate the intricacy and beauty of this process—a myriad of traditions, a collage of identities highlighting the diverse cultural landscape of our global society. Through this appreciation, we reaffirm our commitment to upholding the diversity which fills our world with inspiration, progression, and depth, embodying humanity's vibrant spirit in its full force.

In our ongoing journey delving into this Special Report, we will continue to explore how these stories of tradition and identity manifest in various elements of culture—whether through artifacts, music, dance, or cuisine—unraveling the extraordinary tapestry of our shared human heritage.

Chapter 3. Defining Culture: An Introspective Analysis

Our dynamic exploration kicks off with a deep, introspective dissection of a concept that is as varied and layered as the human experience itself: culture. Culture serves as the cornerstone of our individual and collective identities and anchors us to our shared past while shaping our future pathways. By examining the inherent complexities embedded within the concept of culture, we pave the way for a richer comprehension of our world's diverse traditions and identities.

3.1. Unraveling the Complex Term: Culture

Culture, a concept often taken for granted, is as intricate as a woven tapestry and as multifaceted as the myriad societies it characterizes. It encompasses an array of elements, including values, beliefs, customs, traditions, morals, laws, art, knowledge, and language, among others. It embodies the collective consciousness of a group, shaping the patterns of behavior, thought processes, and emotional responses in turn.

More importantly, culture is a societal mirror that reflects the shared experiences, collective history, and unified narrative of a community. It extends beyond a mere compilation of customary practices. It encapsifies a society's spirit, symbolizing the shared, lived experiences of its members, often handed down through generations. Far from being a static entity, culture is fluid, evolving through time, adapting to changing circumstances, and continuously redefining itself in the context of an increasingly globalized world.

3.2. The Multitudes of Culture: Tangible and Intangible

Culture's manifestations are predominantly categorized into two broad classifications: tangible and intangible. Tangible culture can be physically seen or touched, including artifacts, architecture, clothing, and other physical objects that have cultural significance. For instance, the Great Wall of China or the Statue of Liberty, architectural marvels, carry forward the cultural stories of their respective nations.

On the other hand, intangible culture comprises non-physical aspects, including traditions, language, knowledge, customs, music, dance, myths, and other elements. These forms, although invisible, are equally significant, playing a critical role in preserving our shared human heritage. Take, for example, the riveting story-telling traditions across African societies or the melodious folk songs of Eastern Europe, encapsulating the essence of their respective cultures.

3.3. Dimensions of Culture: The Iceberg Metaphor

Culture tends to operate on two levels, represented metaphorically as an iceberg. The visible or explicit dimension, akin to the iceberg's 'above water' section, includes observable aspects such as language, food, clothing, music, and physical manifestations of art. Meanwhile, the 'below water' section houses the implicit or invisible dimension, made up of unobservable aspects such as beliefs, values, thought patterns, and societal norms.

The iceberg metaphor underscores the complexity of culture by highlighting that the most substantial and influential portions are often hidden beneath the surface levels of visibility. Thus, to understand a culture accurately, one must delve beneath the observable, peeling back the layers to unearth the deeply embedded values, beliefs, and norms forming the cultural core.

3.4. Culture and Identity: A Symbiotic Relationship

The symbiotic relationship between culture and identity is a defining aspect of human society. Culture imbues individuals with a sense of belonging, shaping and expressing their personal and collective identities. It is through the lens of relevant cultural narratives that individuals form their values, beliefs, and behavior, crafting their identity in the process.

Identity, in turn, contributes to culture by weaving the threads of individual experiences, perspectives, and customs into the broader societal fabric. Under this impression, every person paints a unique stroke on the vast cultural canvas, adding a layer of intricate depth to the existing cultural palette.

The harmonious interplay of culture and identity underscores our collective identity as humans, transcending the physical boundaries to bind us together as a global community. It fuels our diverse traditions, forms the crux of our shared narratives, and most importantly, binds us in our shared need for connection, community, and comprehension of our place in the world.

3.5. An Ongoing Dialogue: Culture in an Evolving World

In the face of rapid globalization, the landscape of culture continues to shift dynamically, carrying implications for individual and collective identities worldwide. This dialogue between the old and the new, tradition and change, highlights culture's astounding ability to adapt, evolve, and redefine itself continually.

The proliferation of cross-cultural exchanges leads to cultural assimilation, blending, and diffusion, enriching the cultural confluence and fostering a mutual appreciation of varied traditions and customs. Alongside, it poses challenges, such as potential cultural erosion or homogenization, which call for a balanced approach to safeguarding cultural diversity and preserving our rich cultural heritage.

In the quest to define this complex entity named culture, we journey through layers of shared history, intimate beliefs, strikingly diverse traditions, and captivating rituals that make us uniquely human. By exhaustive introspection and analysis, we begin to grasp the magnitude of the role that culture plays in shaping our identities and traditions, reminding us that while culture may shape us, it is us who shape culture likewise.

Chapter 4. Symbols of Identity: Artifacts, Scripts, and Monuments

Our marvelous journey commences with a gentle notion: our identities are largely defined by the cultural symbols enveloping us. Intricately woven into the fabric of society, these emblems emanate from diverse elements. Some are tangible like artifacts and monuments, while others are abstract, such as scripts. Each component mentioned carries a stunning level of significance, embodying stories, histories, values, and aspirations that culminate into a shared identity. Spanning across various spheres of daily life, they remain at the core of our cultural perception and comprehension.

4.1. Artifacts: Echoes of the Past

Artifacts abound as silent witnesses of a bygone era, echoing past events and practices often shrouded in the misty veil of time. These precious relics encompass a wide range of objects, from everyday utensils and tools to intricate jewelry and ceremonial items, each brimming with tales of yesteryears.

An elaborate appreciation of artifacts takes us, for instance, to the Indus Valley Civilization. The discovery and analysis of their seal, made of steatite, about two square inches in size, intricately carved with animal images and a short inscription, has provided a fascinating look into seals' importance as symbols of authority, exhibiting trade ties and socio-economic statuses.

4.2. Scripts: The Abstract Medium of Expression

Scripts operate as a powerful abstract channel to heritage and identity. They miraculously capture language, the cornerstone of human communication, and store its grandeur for posterity. Comprising distinct symbols, they encapsulate the thought processes and intellectual leanings of their creators, offering invaluable testimony to human civilization's progress.

The Sanskrit language, the oldest language associated with the Indic script, potently symbolizes cultural continuity and Indian heritage. It is the language in which the Vedas, ancient Hindu scriptures, were composed. The sacred script thrives through religious and scholarly usage still today, bearing witness to India's rich linguistic tradition.

4.3. Monuments: Silent Narrators of Epochs

Monuments, the grand architectural feats, stand as silent, colossal narrators of epochs. They ubiquitously symbolize a society's values, struggles, victories, and collective memories. Whether these are awe-inspiring structures like the Pyramids of Egypt, brimming with mystery and tales of a powerful past civilization, or spaces of historical trauma such as the Auschwitz-Birkenau concentration camp, serving as harrowing reminders of the Holocaust, monuments instigate profound contemplation and significance.

Consider the grandeur of the Parthenon in Athens – this iconic Greek masterpiece encapsulates the essence of the Classical period, embodying the cultural, political, and aesthetic ideals of the times. Recently, the arrival of the 3D printing technology has given conservation a new dimension, creating replicas of damaged or destroyed cultural monuments, and breathing new life into our shared cultural heritage.

In conclusion, artifacts, scripts, and monuments together contribute to constructing an elaborate matrix of symbolism intricately defining our identities and connecting us to our roots. They imbibe the essence of our past, perpetuate traditions, and evoke meaningful dialogues about our shared heritage, thereby offering a rich, immersive medium to understand and appreciate the beautiful tapestry of human civilization. As we navigate onwards in our exploration, these symbols remain guiding posts, radiating tradition and identity that are foundational to the entire cultural edifice. Whether tangible or abstract, these are the footprints we, as a race, leave behind—marking our sojourn on the Earth's expansive sands of time.

Chapter 5. Festivities and Rituals: Expressions of Collective Tradition

Every society has a unique cultural lexicon that draws its essence from countless festivities, rituals, and ceremonies celebrated for time immemorial. These manifestations of collective tradition are mirrors into the heart and soul of a societal tapestry, intricately weaving together the past, present, and future in a thematic continuum of shared heritage and identity.

5.1. Celebration - A Universal Impulse

Revelry, it seems, is hardwired into our human DNA, manifesting itself in countless ways across the globe. Throughout history, humans have celebrated the changing seasons, religious beliefs, monumental life events, and significant historical occurrences. Every culture, no matter how remotely located or uniquely practiced, has a system of celebration – a propensity to unite and rejoice, to recollect and anticipate, to reflect and project.

Indeed, these celebrations often manifest as grand spectacles, bursting with bright colours, crisp sounds and euphoric emotions, as can be observed in India's colour-splashed Holi or the rhythmic samba processions of Brazil's Carnival. Yet equally profound are solemn, introspective ceremonies, such as the reflective silence during Japan's Obon festival or the meditative introspection of the Islamic month of Ramadan. These instances expose the dichotomy that exists within the spectrum of human emotion, and underline the importance of balance in our collective cultural mosaic.

5.2. Rituals - Patterns of Practice

Just as essential to our cultural identities are rituals - repeated actions imbued with symbolism and significance that transcend their surface level function. The meticulous procedure of Japanese tea ceremonies, the coming-of-age Maasai warrior initiation, the Aboriginal smoking ceremonies in Australia - these rituals may vary wildly in their nature, but the common thread that binds them all is their ability to pass down teachings, values, and norms from one generation to the next.

Under closer examination, rituals reveal themselves to be far more than simplistic, rigid formulas. They are complex social structures designed to communicate messages, preserve norms, uphold values and perpetuate narratives. Go beyond the aesthetic beauty of the elegant Balinese 'Pendet' dance or the sonorous chants of Tibetan monks, and one begins to understand the decoded messages of unity, harmony, respect, tranquility - fundamental principles upon which societies are built and sustained.

5.3. The Role of Festivities and Rituals

Celebrations and rituals form a constant and marathon relay race of cultural transmission. They carry the burden of the past, the identity of the present and the blueprint of the future. As cultural events, they play a critical role in initiating individuals into the community, affirming their identity, nurturing their societal values, and moulding their perception of the universe and their place in it.

In this way, every Midsummer celebration in Sweden, every Diwali lamp in India, every Christmas carol in England – each serves as a piece of an intricate cultural jigsaw puzzle. Together they form a picture of humanity, rich in diversity yet unified in its shared aspiration for societal cohesiveness, perpetuity, and meaning.

5.4. Transformation and Continuity

Yet, traditions are not static. They are dynamic, living entities that evolve, adapt and transform over time, continuously improvising to fit the narratives of changing times. The incorporation of smartphone applications in the lantern festival in Taiwan, or the use of Zoom for family gatherings during Thanksgiving in the midst of a pandemic, are testaments to this flexibility of traditions.

While technology alters the way we celebrate, the essence of these festivities remains pure, for it is in our collective memory that tradition finds its sanctuary. No matter the medium, the message persists in its tenacity to forge and fortify social bonds, to give meaning to life, and to embrace the paradox of change within continuity.

5.5. Future of Festivities and Rituals

As we journey into the future, our task is two-fold — to preserve these symbols of our cultural heritage, and to allow them to adapt and grow with us. In a world where technology and globalization continuously redefine social paradigms, we must ensure that our traditions don't merely survive but rather, evolve.+

This is not merely an exercise in standing against the winds of cultural erosion, but rather, an active endeavour to chart and navigate the currents of cultural transformation. By tuning the frequencies of tradition to resonate with the beats of the modern world, we can ensure the propagation and preservation of our shared cultural symphony, harmonising the past, the present, and the future.

In its mesmerizing rhythms and resonating echoes, we are reminded of a fundamental truth – that within the diverse expressions of celebration and ritual, we find the image of our collective human identity. These are not just festivities and rituals; they are vibrant threads in our global human tapestry, binding each one of us to the other in a shared dance of collective tradition and individual identity.

We must remember that every tradition kept alive, every ritual faithfully followed, every ancient myth passed down through the ages, all contribute to the grandest epic ever told - the continuous and unfolding saga of humanity. Through the lens of our tradition and identity, we shape the pillars of the future, and create our chapters in the annals of time.

In the grand schema of our shared human history, the festivities and rituals are emblems of unity in diversity, testament to the resilience of the human spirit and the compelling narrative of human accomplishments. They remind us of where we come from, who we are, and where we might be heading. Above all, they bring us together, transcending all boundaries in a celebration of the beautiful kaleidoscope of human existence.

Chapter 6. Dance and Music: A Universal Language of Unity

Beginnings of a Universal Medium === Early Evolutions Some anthropologists and historians suggest that the origins of music and dance are as ancient and primordial as humanity itself. Indeed, even before the advent of language, our ancestors likely used rhythmic movements and melodious vocalizations for communication and ritualistic purposes. These early forms of musical expressions evolved over the centuries, often in tandem with societal and cultural changes. Even physical environments—the rhythms of the waves, the rustle of leaves, or the cacophony of wildlife—likely influenced the development of these primal art forms.

6.1. Dance and Music as Integral Parts of Ancient Cultures

As civilizations formed and flourished, dance and music became ingrained as integral parts of various societies, used for storytelling, spiritual communion, and social bonding. In the ancient Egyptian civilization, for instance, dance and music played a crucial role in religious rituals, celebration ceremonies, and even as a pastime. The wall paintings in Egyptian tombs vividly depict scenes of rhythmic dances, performers playing traditional instruments, and festive musical gatherings.

In similar vein, ancient Greek society implemented music and dance as key components in their cultural fabric. Choral performances were a regular feature in Greek dramas, with melodious accompaniment and strategic bodily movements intensifying the narrative's emotional dynamics.

Tangible Echoes of Identity === Dance: Unspoken Language of the Body Throughout history, dance has been a medium that communicated ideas, desires, and societal norms in a wordless but intense language of the body. Ballet, a form classical dance originating from the Italian Renaissance, later refined in France and Russia, tells intricate stories through technically precise movements. It has been inherently linked with European nobility and elegance. On the other hand, styles such as flamenco, originating from the Andalusian region in Spain, embody the fiery passion, raw emotion and a rich mixture of Romani, Islamic, and Jewish influences.

Similarly, the vast variety of Indian classical dance forms like Bharatanatyam, Kathak, Kathakali, and Odissi are interwoven with Hindu religious mythology and practices. They have been regional symbols of rich tradition and cultural pride.

6.2. Music: Melodic Expression of the Soul

Music, seen across all cultures as a deep-rooted expression of human emotion, also serves as a marker of identity and cohesion. From the hauntingly melancholic ballads of Portuguese Fado to the uplifting beats of Jamaican Reggae, each musical genre encapsulates a unique echo of its origin. The polyphonic harmony of Georgian folk music or the complex rhythmic interplays in traditional West African Djembe drumming reveal the intricate layers of their respective societies. The Irish bagpipes, synonymous with Celtic tradition, ingrained indelibly into the country's identity, speaks volumes about Ireland's tumultuous history and resilient spirit.

Unity in Diversity: A Global Resonance === Transcending Cultural and Geographical Boundaries Once strictly region-specific, dance and music have evolved into forms that transcend cultural and geographical boundaries, becoming a universal language of unity. This has been largely facilitated by technology and globalization.

American Jazz, born out of African-American communities' experiences, is now appreciated around the globe. Salsa, with its Afro-Cuban roots, has found home in dance studios across continents.

6.3. Promoting Understanding and Empathy

Despite their diverse guises, dance and music promote understanding and empathy across cultures. They express universally recognized feelings - joy, sorrow, love, and anger, creating a rich tapestry of human experience. An Alaskan throat singer or an Australian didgeridoo player may perform music impenetrable in language to most, yet the underlying emotion often resonates on a global scale. They serve as visceral reminders of our shared humanity, reinforcing common bonds while simultaneously celebrating the splendid variety of cultural expression.

In an increasingly globalized world, the communal experience of dance and music fosters understanding, challenges prejudices, and ultimately helps blurring the lines that divide us as nations, as cultures, and as individuals. It nurtures a shared sense of unity and belonging - a testament to its all-encompassing power.

Preserving this powerful universal language is crucial. While we embrace a more interconnected world, ensuring the survival of regional dances and music styles, especially those threatened by fading tradition or lack of interest, is indispensable. They represent vital links to our ancestral past and living tributes to human creativity and resilience. By protecting these precious cultural assets, we are not just conserving the integrity of our diverse cultures, but also upholding the harmony, unity, and mutual respect that dance and music so beautifully embody.

Chapter 7. Traditional Gastronomy: A Revealing Lens into Cultural Diversity

As we set out on this stimulating journey of discovery, we first encounter an inescapable truth: food is far more than survival. It is an intricate social artifact, which not only ties us to our individual roots but also reveals a cultural identity that extends as wide as the world itself. So, let's embark on a captivating epicurean voyage, exploring how the diverse world of traditional gastronomy paints a vivid picture of humanity's incredible cultural diversity.

7.1. The Roots of Gastronomy

Our journey commences in the fertile crescent of the Neolithic period, where the advent of agriculture and animal domestication set the stage for the development of early gastronomic practices. Food, for the first time, was not just sustenance but hinted at the possibility of a communal identity connected to shared practices, a means of cultural affiliation. Over epochs, these tendrils of human collective consciousness, driven by geographic, climatic, and socio-political factors, grew and branched out, forming the roots of our diverse gastronomic traditions.

7.2. The Tapestry of Traditional Cuisines

As we journey across continents, one cannot ignore the awe-inspiring array of traditional cuisines. Each regional gastronomic tradition is a kaleidoscope, a beautiful mosaic of flavors that speaks volumes about cultural diversity.

In Asia, take for instance, the richly-spiced Indian curries, the delicate Japanese sushi, or the comforting warmth of Vietnamese pho, each dish is not just a blend of flavors, but a profound reflection of historical narratives, religious beliefs, and societal structures.

In Africa, from the smokey tagine pots of Morocco to the tangy Ugali staple in East Africa, the diverse foodways mirror the continent's great ethnic variance, tying together tales of migration, colonialism, and adaptation.

Europe offers a banquet of culinary diversity, from the pasta and pizza of Italy, the haggis of Scotland, or the fragrant paella of Spain, every dish is enmeshed in history, revealing secrets about trade routes, feudal systems, and even historic struggles for survival.

The Americas, too, display an impressive gastronomic repertoire. Be it the popular Mexican tacos and tamales or the Native American Bison stew, each culinary tradition embeds an echo of the region's native flora, fauna, and historical context.

With every bite we take from these dishes, we are consuming a narrative, a story of culture, tradition, and identity that has endured generations.

7.3. Culinary Practices and Rituals: Stories Behind the Plate

If food is a language, then its vocabulary consists of the methods of cooking, the rituals of eating, and the related practices extending beyond the kitchen. These food practices, like the couscous-steaming women of North Africa or the tea ceremonies in Japan, symbolize community ties, marking respect, love, and unity.

Feasting practices around the world, be it the American Thanksgiving or the Maori Hangi, embody the spirit of collective joy, gratitude, and community bonding. Additionally, food taboos and dietary restrictions often seen in religious observances, such as fasting during Ramadan or the prohibition of pork in Judaism, delineate social boundaries and reinforce cultural identity.

7.4. The Spice Trade: A Story of Cultural Interactions

The far-reaching effects of the spice trade in expanding the global culinary landscape is worth noting here. This age-old economic endeavor spurred cultural exchange, fostering culinary innovation and diversity. Imagine Italian cuisine without tomatoes, brought over from the Americas, or Indian food without the fiery chillies, originally from Mexico.

7.5. Traditional Gastronomy: Ecology and Sustainability

Another lens through which traditional gastronomy can be understood pertains to ecology and sustainability. Many indigenous communities have developed food practices that respect and conserve nature. For instance, the forest-to-table traditions of the Amazonian tribes or the sustainable farming practices of the Balinese.

7.6. Securing Gastronomy's Future: Challenges & Resolutions

Our gastronomic journey would be incomplete without discussing challenges and proposed resolutions. The homogenizing force of globalization threatens to dilute these culinary traditions. Fast food culture pushes palates towards homogeneity, risking the loss of our richly diverse food heritage.

Yet, there are glimmers of hope seen in movements like Slow Food and public recognition platforms like UNESCO's intangible cultural heritage list that aim to protect and promote traditional gastronomy, preserving it for future generations.

In closing, traditional gastronomy truly is a revealing lens into cultural diversity. It maps our collective histories, encodes our values, and hints at our shared futures. In delving into the breadth and depth of our world's culinary heritage, we encounter the soul of cultures, providing us with a richer understanding of the human story. Our journey through the rich landscape of traditional gastronomy underpins an axiom: nourishment consists of more than just the food on a plate. It involves cherished memories, revered rituals, and human connectedness embedded in our edible traditions.

Chapter 8. Language and Literature: Carriers of Cultural Identity

Language, as an inherent component of culture, has been one of the fundamental hallmarks of human civilization, facilitating communication, concentrating shared knowledge, and playing an instrumental role in community cohesion. Substantially more profound than merely a conduit for dialogue or exchange, language's intrinsic links to cultural identity, heritage, and historical imprint cannot be overstated. As a living expression of a society's worldview, it encapsulates a collective's history, traditions, rituals, beliefs, and ideas. Literature yields similar effects, elevating language to an art form, embodying a culture's essence through its motifs and themes, and chronicling the nuances of human lives, experiences, and imaginations across time and space.

8.1. On the Cultural Implications of Language

One may initialize this intricate exploration by scrutnizing the cultural implications of language. Language is an extraordinary chronicle of cultural evolution, encapsulating histories—both societal and communal, expressing social mores, and endorsing shared values and folklore. Its lexicon often delineates the social, economic, and environmental aspects of the culture it represents. For instance, the Inuit language, spoken by the indigenous people of the Arctic regions, includes an extensive vocabulary related to snow and ice, mirroring the centrality of these elements to their survival and identity. By contrast, the Polynesian languages have an extensive nautical vocabulary, reflecting their seafaring tradition.

The grammar and structure of a language can also provide insights into a society's social structure and ideology. For example, many indigenous American languages display a high level of complexity in their verb systems, which may reflect a cultural emphasis on action and process. Some languages, such as Korean or Japanese, incorporate honorifics into their grammar, commenting on the society's emphasis on status and hierarchy.

8.2. Literature: A Reflection of Cultural Nuances

The connection between literature and cultural identity is an equally fascinating subject of exploration. Literature broadens the scope of language, converting it into an art form that illustrates a culture's emotional landscape, social philosophies, and historical narrative. Texts from different eras and regions offer an intriguing insight into the societal norms, values, conflicts, and transformations that have characterized different periods in history.

From the epic poems of Homer, which encapsulate ancient Greek philosophy and worldview, to the haikus of Matsuo Basho, reflecting Japan's Zen Buddhist tradition and appreciation for nature's transient beauty, or even the contemporary novels exploring post-colonial identity crises—literature serves as a cultural mirror, where a society's nerves are most candidly touched upon.

8.3. The Interplay of Language and Literature

Symbiotically, language and literature operate in a space of mutual influence. The words, idioms, and stylistic choices available in a language can shape literature produced in that language, influencing the themes and styles adopted by authors. Conversely, literature often acts as a catalyst for language evolution. By promoting new vocabulary, idioms, or stylistic devices, authors can stimulate linguistic development, demonstrating language's dynamic nature.

Shakespeare, for instance, is accredited with coining several words and phrases in English. In the Tagore era, Bengali literature underwent significant evolution, which had a profound impact on the Bengali language as well. Similarly, the works of James Joyce are renowned for their innovation in English diction and syntax.

8.4. Language Disruption, Endangerment, and Revitalization

From the destruction of the Library of Alexandria to the linguistic repercussions of colonialism, the changing course of history has often led to language endangerment and even extinction—an unfortunate reality that threatens cultural diversity. Today, linguistic experts express concerns over many languages teetering on the brink of extinction. As these languages disappear, so does an irreplaceable piece of the world's cultural mosaic, and the unique worldview they represent.

However, a counter-wave of language revitalization efforts has been taking shape around the globe, with cultural communities rallying to rescue their linguistic legacies. These endeavors range from the revival of Welsh in the United Kingdom to the preservation of Ainu in Japan, illuminating a collective consciousness regarding the value of linguistic heritage.

8.5. Literature's Role in Preserving Cultural Identity

Equipped with an underlying narrative power, literature often steps in as a powerful ally in the battle for cultural preservation. It documents and perpetuates traditions, folklores, philosophical ideas, societal norms, and historical narratives, playing a crucial role in maintaining a sense of continuity and integrity to a culture's identity.

On the other hand, literature can also be an effective tool in challenging prevailing norms and catalyzing societal change. From Chinua Achebe's critique of colonialism in "Things Fall Apart" to Margaret Atwood's exploration of female agency in "The Handmaid's Tale," literature is not merely a preserver but also a questioner of cultural practices, exemplifying its multifaceted role in shaping identity.

Thus, scrutinizing the interplay of language and literature in the context of cultural identity uncovers an enriching landscape of historical narratives, societal values, philosophical dialogues, and emotional landscapes. As much as they shape our societies and perceptions, they themselves are shaped by us - making them living, breathing entities, chronicling humanity's struggles, triumphs, and ceaseless quest for self-expression.

Chapter 9. Traditional Clothing: A Tapestry of Time and Identity

From the Stone Age's simple animal skin wraps, through the elaborate court dresses of the European Renaissance, to the tailored suits found in modern metropolises, traditional clothing stands as a vivid testament to the inexorable passage of time entwined with ingrained cultural identity. Serving purposes beyond mere coverage and comfort, these garments arise from the intricate looms of societal norms, values, history and local geographic conditions, shaping and reflecting the identity of the people wearing them.

9.1. The Significance of attire: An Intimate Connection to Identity

Clothing is not only an attire but a rich narrative, a voice echoing the tales of ancestors, a visible manifestation of an individual's or a community's identity. Each stitching pattern, color chosen, and material used is demonstrative of its wearers' beliefs, traditions, and status. In a nutshell, clothing is physical evidence of the intangible cultural aura beneath, offering a silent yet profound commentary on society's milestones and evolution.

9.2. Evolution of Traditional Clothing: Chronicles from the Hands of Time

Tracing the evolution of traditional clothing reveals pages of world history. For instance, the 'Hanbok' of Korea speaks volumes about their Confucian society, placing emphasis on simplicity and modesty. Meanwhile, the 'Sari' of South India has evolved over centuries, with variations reflecting shifts in societal norms and external influences. Deep dives into the transformation of traditional outfits offer a captivating journey through history, sharpening our appreciation of humanity's rich and colorful tapestry.

9.3. The Vocabulary of Colors and Motifs

Colors and motifs are living lexicons, speaking volumes beyond their visual appeal. Colors in traditional clothing often symbolize certain societal aspects. For instance, white symbolizes purity in many cultures, whereas black usually showcases mourning or respect. Furthermore, motifs provide additional layers of meaning. In many communities, different motifs symbolize varying elements of life, local beliefs, or historical events, thereby serving as visual documentation of societal evolution.

9.4. Championing Local Material: A Testament to Geographic Conditions and Innovation

The materials used for traditional clothing reveal the symbiosis between humans and their environment. For instance, the Scots' kilts were made of wool to withstand the harsh Highlands' cold, and the Pacific Islanders' tapa cloth was derived from local barks, demonstrating their innovative utilitarian usage of available resources.

9.5. Traditional Clothing as Socioeconomic Indicators

Interestingly, traditional clothing also serves as socioeconomic indicators, with variations in fabric, ornamentation, and design often evidencing the wearer's social standing and economic capacity. From the ermine fur in royal cloaks to the extensive beading in Native American outfits, these details offer insightful glimpses into societal hierarchy and economic disparity.

9.6. The Modern Age: Catalyst of Changes and Adaptations

However, with the rise of globalization, traditional clothing has faced shifts. Western-style clothing's popularity has impacted even the most remote corners of the world, leading to questions about tradition and modernity. Yet, somehow, amidst this shifting landscape, traditional clothing has found ways to persist, and in some instances, even evolve, taking on new forms while staying true to its roots.

9.7. Preserving Traditional Clothing: An Imperative Task

Preservation of traditional clothing is crucial as it carries immeasurable cultural value and tangible heritage. Efforts worldwide to restore and renew interest in conventional garments have taken various forms, from integrating traditional elements into modern fashion, dedicated museum exhibitions, to interactive, community-based initiatives vested in retaining this treasured cultural identity.

In our journey across the centuries, we've unraveled the complex threads of traditional clothing, immensely instrumental in binding a community's identity. These cherished embodiments of heritage, their nuanced language of colors, motifs, and materials, down to their transformations in the face of modernity, tightly weave the tale of humanity that continues to evolve and adapt. As we walk towards the future, it becomes more essential than ever to recognize and appreciate these visual artifacts of our cultural tapestry, sustaining these enduring styles for generations to come.

Chapter 10. Clash and Fusion: The Impact of Globalization on Traditions

The epochal advent of globalization, a phenomenon fueled by advancements in technology, travel, and communication, has had a far-reaching impact on the traditions of communities across the globe. As the tapestry of distinctive cultures intertwines in the face of globalized systems, the resultant interaction has catalyzed a fascinating landscape of tradition clash and fusion.

10.1. The Onrush of Globalization

The onset of globalization stands as a testament to the unfettered llimitations of human progress. As technological advancements shrunk the vast expanse of our world, cultures previously miles apart needed to grapple with the proximity precipitated by this evolvement. In essence, globalization became the stage upon which cultural traditions were propelled into unprecedented rounds of interaction, sparking both synergies and clashes that reverberated across the varied facets of societies.

These international collisions of culture were met with an interesting array of reactions. In many instances, communities held steadfast, vying to preserve their heritage in its purest form to resist the seemingly onslaught of a pervasive global culture. In contrast, several cultures embraced globalization's tide, participating in exchanges that blended traditions, resulting in a fusion of customs and practices.

10.2. Tradition Clash: The Rumble of Cultures

Tradition clash is an offshoot of opposing cultural viewpoints born from globalization. The advent of global communication systems paves the way for a continual stream of alien ideas, customs, and beliefs into the parochial landscape of any society. Over time, these external influences begin to challenge and sometimes alter the ingrained cultural practices, evoking a sense of discord or unease amongst a society's custodians and bearers of traditions.

The layers of tension caused by such clashes, however, are multifaceted. On the one hand, it poses an existential threat to cultural identity, traditions, languages, and practices – often prompting a wave of cultural preservation efforts or rising xenophobia. On the other hand, the confrontation of cultures can lead to a transformative evolution - a re-assessment and, in some instances, refinement of long-practiced traditions.

10.3. Tradition Fusion: The Melting Pot of Globalization

The other facet of globalization's impact on traditions is the fusion of cultures. The borders of traditional practices may blur as they adapt to or adopt elements from a different cultural context. Such intermingling often results in a medley of traditional practice – a salad bowl where elements of multiple cultures co-exist to create enriched, multi-layered experiences.

This blending of traditions is most vividly experienced in the realms of cuisine, fashion, music, and dance. For instance, jazz music – a profoundly expressional embodiment of American culture – is a fusion involving African rhythms, European chord structure, and uniquely American spirit. Similarly, Indian curry's popularity across the globe has led to a fusion cuisine, with 'currywurst' in Germany or the 'kedgeree' in the United Kingdom becoming illustrative examples.

10.4. The Fine Balance

Despite the impacts and sometimes tumultuous reconfigurations resulting from globalization, it's important to remember that such encounters between traditions can be enriching and transformative. Clash could drive societal introspection and progress, and fusion could present more vibrant and inclusive expressions of tradition.

Regardless, the key lies in striking a delicate balance. The preservation of cultural identities and traditions is vital. Still, these structures must be permeable insofar as they can adapt, evolve, and change to incorporate lessons and beauty from other cultures: a testament to humanity's ability to grow collectively.

10.5. The Unfolding Chapter

In conclusion, globalization has undeniably shaped the way traditions interact and evolve in our ever-more connected society. Cultures can clash or meld, yielding a landscape that is multifaceted, resilient, and continually adapting. The influence of globalization on our traditions will continue to challenge and shape us in ways we can foresee, as well as in ways still to unravel. After all, we are navigating a living, evolving planet that thrives on and cherishes diversity while attempting to find unity amongst its inhabitants.

Chapter 11. A Cultural Voyage: Preserving Tradition and Identity for the Future

Casting our eyes across the grand expanse of human history, it is clear that cultures have always been fluid, constantly changing, and adapting in response to new influences and circumstances. But in our present era of increasing globalization and rapid technological progress, many are concerned that traditional cultures, and the identities they imbue, are under threat, on the brink of being whitewashed by a monolithic, global culture. However, it is equally possible that we stand on the precipice of new opportunities for preserving and even revitalizing traditions and identities, harnessing the mantle of innovation to safeguard the customs of yore.

11.1. The Peril of Global Homogenization

The advent of globalization has brought about unprecedented levels of cross-cultural exchange. While this has built bridges of understanding between people from a myriad of different backgrounds, it simultaneously poses a threat to the preservation of unique cultural identities. Intrinsic elements of individual cultures can potentially become diluted in the melee of the global cultural marketplace. International trade, travel, and communication systems are often dominated by western practices, leading to a phenomenon known as 'cultural imperialism'. This process can engender a sense of cultural loss amongst communities, particularly those that are smaller or less globally influential.

11.2. The Power of Modern Technologies

Despite the challenges posed by globalization, modern technologies also offer unprecedented opportunities to preserve and even revitalize cultural traditions. Today's digital tools can capture and reproduce human cultural expressions in high fidelity detail. From digital libraries housing thousands of scanned ancient manuscripts to virtual reality experiences that transport users to historical landmarks or traditional cultural events, technology is providing new avenues for bringing our cultural heritage to life and ensuring its continuation for generations to come. Moreover, these technologies allow cultures to present themselves on their own terms, resisting the cultural homogenization imposed by dominant cultures and carving out space for the continued existence and evolution of all world cultures.

11.3. Grassroots Movements and Institutional Support

At the same time, various means of preserving tradition and identity are emerging from communities and institutional bodies across the globe. Grassroots movements around the world are focused on the revitalization of cultural traditions, with an emphasis on passing them down to the next generation through regular practice and instruction. Festivals and events celebrating communal traditions are growing in popularity, in part due to heightened global interest in unique cultural phenomena. Concurrently, international bodies like UNESCO have begun recognizing the importance of preserving intangible cultural heritage alongside physical sites, highlighting the growing awareness of the importance of cultural preservation in the face of increasing globalization.

11.4. The Role of Education

Education plays a pivotal role in combating cultural erosion by instilling a sense of respect and appreciation for one's own cultural traditions as well as those of others. Infusing curricula with comprehensive material about local and global cultures, their histories, their strengths, and the challenges they face, not only induces a broader understanding but also nurtures a pluralistic perspective amongst learners. Including folklore, literature, language, and history in educational content can also allow younger generations to feel the continuum of tradition, bridging the gap between past, present, and future.

11.5. Shaping the Future with Tradition and Identity

As we embark on a journey through the 21st century, it is crucial to remember that tradition and identity, far from being relics of the past, are vibrant and living repositories of human experience. They color our worldview, guide our interactions, and offer a sense of belonging and stability amidst change. The tools and resources for safeguarding these invaluable assets are at our disposal. In the era of globalization and technology, we must become active participants in this preservation process, fostering a global community that celebrates diversity, deepens understanding, and enriches our shared human narrative.